for Julie Rosenfeld, in warm friendship

DUO FOR VIOLIN AND PIANO
IN ONE MOVEMENT

KENNETH FUCHS

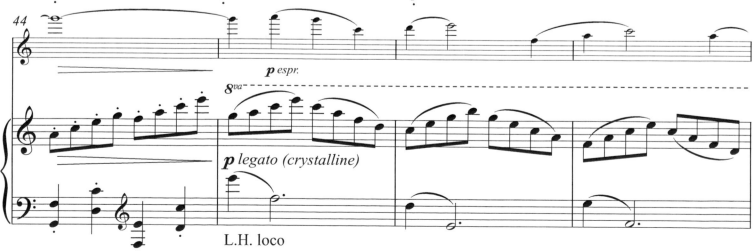

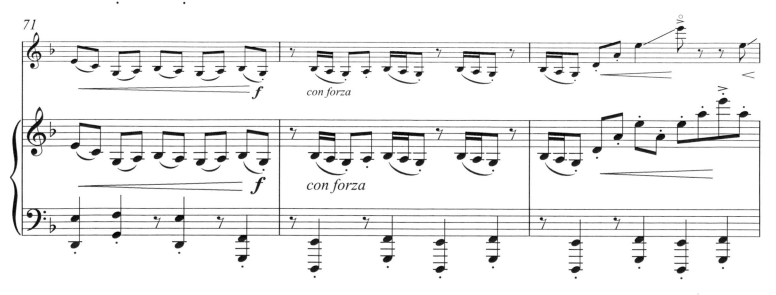

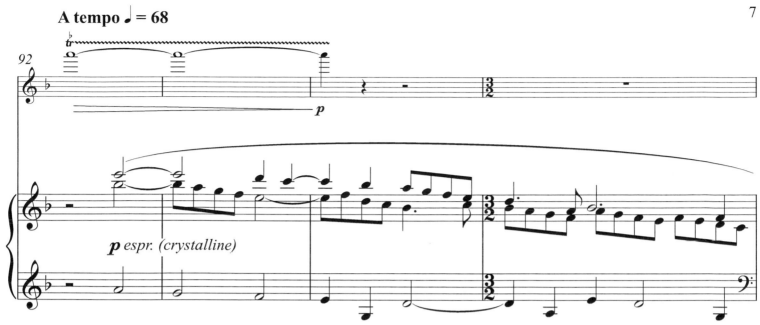

8

Violin

for Julie Rosenfeld, in warm friendship

DUO FOR VIOLIN AND PIANO
IN ONE MOVEMENT

KENNETH FUCHS

Violin

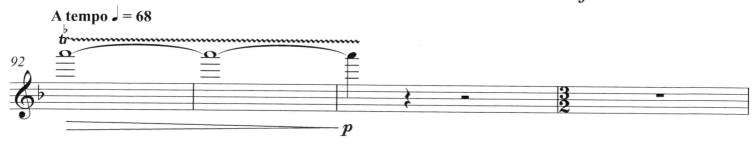

Allegro scherzando ♩ = 136

Violin

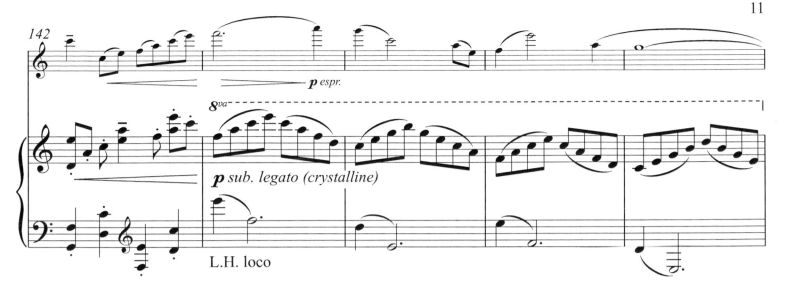

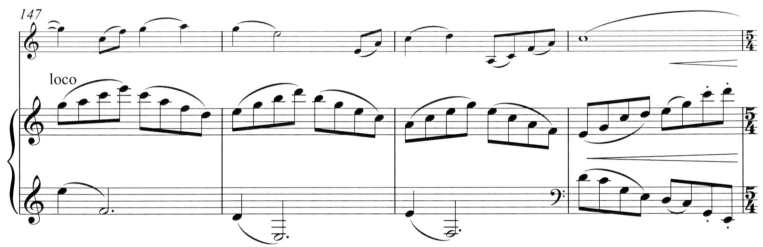

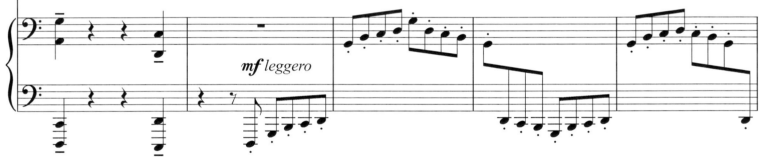

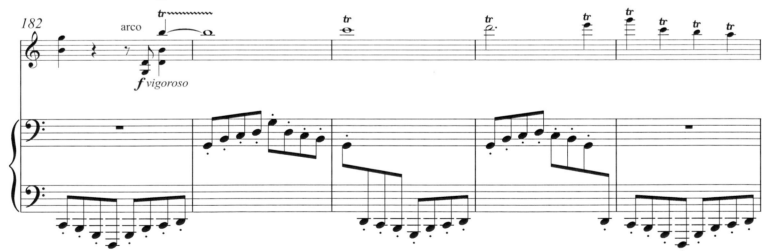

14

poco agitato al meas. 205